My Dog

My Dog

Heidi Goennel

Orchard Books
A division of Franklin Watts, Inc.
New York

Orchard Books   Orchard Books Canada
A division of Franklin Watts, Inc.   20 Torbay Road
387 Park Avenue South   Markham, Ontario 23P 1G6
New York, NY 10016

Manufactured in the United States of America
Book design by Heidi Goennel and Martha Rago

10 9 8 7 6 5 4 3 2 1

The text of this book is set in 24 point Palatino Bold
The illustrations are acrylic paint on canvas

Library of Congress Cataloging-in-Publication Data
Goennel, Heidi.   My dog / Heidi Goennel.   p. cm.   Summary: A little girl enumerates the many kinds of dogs she likes, including cocker spaniel, collie, and sheepdog, but confesses she loves her own best.
ISBN 0-531-05834-4.–ISBN 0-531-08434-5 (lib. bdg.)
1. Dogs–Juvenile literature. [1. Dogs.] I. Title. SF426.5.G64 1989
636.7–dc19   88-38706   CIP   AC

To Peter

I like a dog with deep dark eyes

like a cocker spaniel.

I like a dog with a nose as soft as a pug.

I like a dog with a great loud bark
like a German shepherd.

I like a dog with long floppy ears
like a basset hound.

I like a dog who has a silky coat like a collie.

I like a dog who can fetch and play
like a beagle.

I like a dog who is as big as a pony,

like a Saint Bernard.

I like a dog who can swim very fast

like a Labrador.

I like a dog with a soft white tummy
like a sheepdog.

I like a dog with tall, tall legs like a Great Dane.

I like a dog who is as tiny as a kitten,
like a Chihuahua.

But most of all, I like *my* dog.

He's just a little brown dog.

But I love him so.